Introduction

Passed on orally from at least the first century BC the Brehon Laws, named for Ireland's wandering jurists, were first set down on parchment in the seventh century AD, using the newly-developed, written Irish language, and continued in use until the beginning of the seventeenth century.

Although the Irish had been living by the laws since before the time of Julius Caesar, by the time of Elizabeth I the Brehons, along with the Irish poets, were considered a danger to the realm, and the old laws 'lewd', 'unreasonable', and 'barbarous'. And so the Brehons, the poets and the ancient laws were banned and English common law substituted. It was the end of the Gaelic order.

Some of the Brehons buried their precious manuscripts, or hid them behind loose stones in the hearth. Other manuscripts became torn or damp, and were burned or allowed to rot. Fortunately, a good number of manuscripts fell into the hands of collectors, and are now safe in the libraries of Trinity College and the Royal Irish Academy in Dublin, at the British Museum, Oxford University and on the continent of Europe.

In 1852 the Brehon Law Commission employed two

native Irish scholars, Eugene O'Curry and John O'Donovan, to unravel the mysteries of the laws. For years they poured over the manuscripts. Sitting in dimly-lit libraries, surrounded by pens and ink-pots, every day they peered through magnifying glasses at the handwriting of the old scribes, struggling to decipher the tiny glosses that ran between the lines and up the margins. For clarity they first copied the laws onto fresh sheets of paper. Then they translated them into English.

What gradually came to light as, in the words of D. A. Binchy, 'the crabbed and obscure texts. . . yielded up their secrets', was not simply a collection of dry and dusty prohibitions, but thousands of details – details that describe ancient life in the days when the Irish still lived in mud huts and small ringed settlements, and paid their bills in cows and bacon, handsome gold brooches and ordinary wooden bowls: the brewer testing a grain of malt against his tooth to guard against bitterness in the ale; farmers lugging sides of beef to the chieftain, to pay their quarterly rent; a pregnant wife who craves a morsel of food; mischievous boys shouting at pigs.

Myles Dillon has called the Irish law-tracts 'probably the most important documents of their kind in the whole tradition of western Europe.' The value lies not only in their great antiquity, or in the pictures of everyday life unavailable from other sources. It may lie primarily in the fact that the Irish Celts, unlike those of France and Britain, were never conquered by Rome. Instead, Ireland had grown up in what some like to call 'splendid isolation' across the Irish sea.

So the Irish laws serve as a repository of primitive customs, some dating back 3,000 years and most gathered by Celtic wanderers from various members of the far-flung Indo-European family.

Certain Irish laws, for example, mirror the Germanic tribal custom of demanding payment of a fine, generally in livestock, for deliberate assault or homicide. Others outline preparations for the great assemblies held regularly at Tara and other pagan burial sites long before the arrival of Patrick – gatherings that correspond to the assemblies and funeral games held at the Roman Forum. Scholars could conceivably compare the strong position of women in the Irish laws with that of women in Greece at the time of Homer.

Perhaps the Hindu procedure of sitting *dharna* most dramatically reveals the ancient Indo-European connections: a creditor, particularly one of a lower class than the recalcitrant debtor, was entitled to sit in front of the debtor's house daily and fast, to embarrass the debtor into paying up.

Other laws, such as the Irish 'blush-fine' for unjustly satirizing a fellow tribesman, demonstrate the dread of losing face, a fear shared with the ancient Irish by such widely scattered societies as the Japanese, and the Ashanti tribespeople of Ghana. Moreover, the Brehon Laws often remind Jews of the *Talmud*, and other scholars of pre-Islamic Arab traditions.

Although scholars have called the old Irish laws 'gravely defective' in that they were not based on principles or never produced a central organization, Eoin MacNeill wrote in 1934 that even Ireland's enemies in the time of Elizabeth and James I commented on the love of the Irish for justice, and for their laws. I, for one, can see why.

THE GREAT TRIBAL ASSEMBLY AT CARMAN

The Feis

'There they discussed and debated
the rights and taxes of the province:
every legal enactment right piously,
every third year it was settled.'

from The Poem of Carman

(11th century)

Every third year roads must be cleared of brambles, weeds and water to prepare for the great assembly.

The harpist is the only musician
who is of noble standing.
Flute-players, trumpeters and timpanists,
as well as jugglers, conjurers and equestrians who
stand on the backs of horses at fairs, have no status
of their own in the community, only that of the noble
chieftain to whom they are attached.

The creditor who holds your brooch, your necklet
or your earrings as a pledge against your loan must
return them so you may wear them
at the great assembly.
Or he will be fined for your humiliation.

Speech is given to three:
to the historian-poet for the narration
and relating of tales,
to the poet-seer for praise and satire,
and to the Brehon for giving judgement.

The time allotted to each Brehon for pleading his case
is long or short according to his dignity.
In determining the length of the speech he is allowed,
count eighteen breathings to the minute.

When a judge deviates from the truth a blotch
will appear on his cheek.

On the best land everything is good. The herbs are
sweet and no manure or shells are needed. There will
be no plants that will stick in a horse's mane or tail:
no briars, no blackthorns, no burdocks.

For the best arable land the price is twenty-four cows.
The price for dry, coarse land is twelve dry cows.

How many things add to the price of land?
A wood, a mine, the site of a mill, a highway, a road,
a great sea, a river, a mountain, a river falling
into the sea, a cooling pond for cattle.
Add three cows to the price if it is near a chieftain's
house or a monastery.

For stripping the bark of an oak tree, enough to tan
the leather for a pair of woman's shoes,
the fine is one cow-hide.
The defendant must cover the bruised portion with
a mixture of wet clay, new milk and cow-dung.

If a man takes a woman off on a horse, into the woods or onto a sea-going ship, and if members of the woman's tribe are present, they must object within twenty-four hours or they may not demand payment of the fine.

The husband-to-be shall pay a bride-price of land,
cattle, horses, gold or silver to the father of the bride.
Husband and wife retain individual rights to
all the land, flocks and household goods
each brings to the marriage.

The husband who, through listlessness, does not go
to his wife in her bed must pay a fine.

If a pregnant woman craves a morsel of food and her husband withholds it through stinginess or neglect, he must pay a fine.

Children shall be sent at an early age to distant
members of the tribe to be reared in the hereditary
professions of law, medicine, poetic composition
or war, or of tilling the soil and wifeliness.
Foster children shall be returned to their parents
at the marriage age: fourteen for girls
and seventeen for boys.

If a woman makes an assignation with a man to come
to her in a bed or behind a bush, the man is not
considered guilty even if she screams.
If she has not agreed to a meeting, however,
he is guilty as soon as she screams.

If the chief wife scratches the concubine but it is out
of rightful jealousy that she does it,
she is exempt from liability for injury.
The same does not hold true for injuries
by the concubine.

Six cows are the fine for breaking a tribesman's
two front teeth; twelve heifers, for maiming
a homeless man.
For pulling off the hairs of a virgin bishop the fine
is one yearling heifer for every twenty hairs.

The doctor shall build his house over a running stream.
His house must not be slovenly or smeared
with the tracks of snails.
It must have four doors that open out so the patients
may be seen from every side at all times.

No fools, drunks or female scolds are allowed in the doctor's house when a patient is healing there. No bad news to be brought, and no talking across the bed. No grunting of pigs or barking of dogs outside.

If the doctor heals your wound, but it breaks out anew
because of his carelessness, neglect or gross want
of skill, he must return the fee you paid.
He must also pay you damages as if he himself
had wounded you.

Whoever comes to your door, you must feed him or care for him, with no questions asked.

It is illegal to give someone food in which has been
found a dead mouse or weasel.

The chief poet of the tribe shall sit next to the king at a banquet. Each shall be served the choicest cut of meat.

The poet who overcharges for a poem shall be stripped of half his rank in society.

Cows, pigs, horses, sheep, goats,
dogs, cats, hens, geese – noisy goods!
Little bees that stick to all flowers.
These are the ten beasts
of all the world's men.
(The Chieftain who is keeper of the free public hostel
must have one hundred of all of these.)

The hostel-keeper must own a cauldron large enough
to boil a pig and a cow at the same time.
Before taking the meat out of the boiling cauldron
the attendant must warn, 'Stand back – here goes the
fleshfork into the cauldron!'

A layman may drink six pints of ale with his dinner, but a monk may drink only three pints. This is so he will not be intoxicated when prayer-time arrives.

The feller of trees must warn all within shouting
distance before he takes the first blow.
All beasts, blind persons and people dozing
must be removed from the area.

If an accident occurs while a building is under
construction no fine is due for injury to the bystander
who is present only out of curiosity.
Should the owners of the building have knowledge
of danger or defect, however, full payment shall be
made to those present on legitimate business,
and to beasts.
(But only half payment to idlers.)

The blacksmith must rouse all sleeping customers
before he puts the iron in the fire.
This is to guard against injuries by sparks.
*Those who fall asleep again will receive
no compensation for injuries.*

If the head of the blacksmith's hammer flies off the handle and injures a customer, neither the smith nor the striker of the hammer is liable – *unless they knew the head was loose.*

If a chip of wood from the carpenter's axe hits
a bystander the carpenter is exempt from liability
unless he deliberately aimed the chip at the bystander.

The mill-owner is exempt from liability for injury
to a person caught between the mill-stones.

If your land has neither fence nor stone wall
you must restrain your beasts lest they damage
your neighbour's property.
For goats a shoe of leather goes on each leg,
for yearling calves put on a spancel. The pig,
which does the most damage of all, must wear a yoke.

The fine for the hen's trespass into the neighbour's
herb garden is one oat-cake plus a side-dish
of butter or bacon.
To keep your hen at home you shall tie a withe
around her feet.

If your neighbour does not repay the debt
he owes you, you may prevent him from going
about his daily business.
A withe-tie (for all to see) goes on the blacksmith's
anvil, the carpenter's axe or the tree-feller's hatchet.
He is on his honour to do no work until he has
righted the wrong.

If the poet or the physician is in debt, immobilize
his horse-whip, for both ride their circuits
on the backs of horses.

Five-fold are crimes:
the crime of the hand, by wounding or stealing;
the crime of the foot, by kicking or moving
to do evil deeds;
the crime of the tongue, by satire, slander
or false witness;
the crime of the mouth, by eating stolen things;
the crime of the eye, by watching while an evil deed
is taking place.

The fine for killing a bond-person held as security
for a loan (or for killing a slave) is twenty-one cows;
for killing a free farmer of Erin
the fine is forty-two cows.
For killing a noble the fine for homicide is paid,
plus an additional amount determined by
his rank in society.
Fines are doubled for malice aforethought.

For stealing your pigs or your sheep, for stripping
your herb garden, for wearing down your hatchet
or wood-axe, you may take your neighbour's
milk cows to the public animal pound for three days.
If he does not want his cows taken to the pound
for his crimes or his bad debts, he may give
his son as security instead.

Blush-fines are payable for insults offered to all
persons of every rank except the ne'er-do-well,
the squanderer, the selfish man who thinks only
of his cows and his fields (and not of other people),
the buffoon who distorts himself before crowds
at a fair and the professional satirist.

Notice of the hound in heat and the mad dog must be sent to the four nearest neighbourhoods.

If a dog commits a nuisance on a neighbour's land the dog's ordure must be removed as far as its juice is found. The ground must be pressed and stamped upon by the heel, and fine clay put there to cover it. Compensation shall be paid in butter, dough or curds amounting to three times the size of the ordure.

The lender of a horse must give notice
of the horse's kicking habits.

Three days is the stay of your cattle in the pound
for a quarrel in the ale-house, injury of thy chief,
over-working a valuable horse, maiming thy chained
dog, disturbing a fair or a great assembly, or striking
or violating thy wife.

Five days for satirizing a man after his death.

If a youth incites a pig by shouting at it for sport,
and the pig charges at idlers in the farmyard,
the pig is exempt from liability for injuries.

February first is the day on which husband or wife
may decide to walk away from the marriage.

The fine for peering into your neighbour's house
without permission is one cow.
For taking a handful of straw off his thatched roof,
one calf is the penalty.

If a rational adult brings a simpleton into an ale-house
just to amuse the patrons, and if the noise and
excitement cause the simpleton to injure another
patron, the adult who brought him there
must make compensation.

If you see a horse straying near a river in the dark,
or a pit, and do nothing to save it,
you must make restitution.

When you become old your family must provide you
with one oatcake a day, plus a container of sour milk.
They must bathe you every twentieth night
and wash your head every Saturday.
Seventeen sticks of firewood is the allotment
for keeping you warm.

Notes

pages 43 and 44: a withe is a strip of flexible willow.

page 49: a blush-fine was a fine payable for causing embarrassment.

page 55: like concubinage, divorce was legal in Ireland until the twelfth century.